MW01701391

"Victoria Boston has done it again! *3 Slow Nickels* is a story that you have to read when you want to be inspired and know exactly how to live your best life."

—Jonathan Sprinkles
Voted one of America's Top Speakers,
Author of multiple #1 Amazon Best sellers, Television Personality,
Founder of Presentation Power

"*3 Slow Nickels* will take you on a journey of success, filled with real- life disappointments, challenges, and adversity, yet provide practical advice and simple truth on how to overcome. After reading this book, you will walk away truly inspired and filled with hope so that you also, will become your best self and an inspiration to others."

—Coach Clint Crouch
Founder of Skills Society; former Assistant Coach for WNBA's Washington Mystics and Director of Camps & Clinics Division of the NBA's Washington Wizards

"Victoria Boston has wonderful advice for anyone looking for success in family, career, and life overall! Never handed a silver spoon, she built an amazing life and one that you too can have. *3 Slow Nickels* will inspire you and provide golden nuggets on how to do just that. Take the journey with her!"

—Kim Gandy
President of National Network to End Domestic Violence (NNEDV)

"Vicky Boston has real stories to tell and keeps it real in the process. Having overcome and beat the odds, she gives it to you straight and provokes self-determination. She inspires greatness in those around her and remains grateful and humble along the way. *3 Slow Nickels* is a must read! "

—Andrea Custis
Former Group President, Verizon Advanced Services

"Vicky Boston is that rare leader that brings the true potential out of her team through her unwavering personal courage, relentless pursuit of excellence, and unmatched ability to inspire employees at every level. While many leaders are busy "talking the talk", Vicky leads her team from the trenches, coaching her team through tough times, and celebrating success each step of the way. Vicky Boston is an inspiration and I am a better leader, husband, and father because of her influence on my life. You want to read *3 Slow Nickels*."

—Chris Arnold
Director of Operations, Verizon Wireless
Former Vice President of Alltel Communications

3 SLOW NICKELS

11/16/25
Happy BIG 95 Aunt Laura!
♡
Love you
Vicky B
♡

Copyright © 2025 by Victoria Boston

This book is available at quantity discounts for bulk purchases.

All rights reserved. No part of this book may be reproduced or transmitted in any form or by any means, electronic or mechanical, including photocopying, recording, or any information storage and retrieval system, without written permission of the publisher except for brief quotations used in reviews, written specifically for inclusion in newspapers, blogs, or magazines.

Stock images: Veer.com

ISBN-13: 978-0-9979635-9-5

Printed in the United States of America

WWW.EDITANDPUBLISH.COM
E&P BOOKS

Dedication

To my amazing parents,
Ellsworth "Hutch" & Louise Daniel Hutchinson

I couldn't have been more blessed to have you as incredible examples growing up. Now that you're shining bright among the heavenly stars, I'm deeply grateful that you continue to guide my footsteps and watch over me. You continue to, and will always be, a source of strength and inspiration in all that I do.

Table of Contents

Introduction

to the 10th Anniversary Edition

Photo: #HutchinsonStrong. Celebrating Hutch's 95th Birthday, November 2022

I am still in shock that it's been a full decade since I first shared *3 Slow Nickels* with the world. I had no idea it would quickly become an international bestseller in Canada and Germany, and among the top 10 in the United States. It was something I never imagined or dared to dream. I only wrote the book to please my dad, who made the request or, should I say, politely made the demand!

After my mom's transition in 2014, my father suggested that I write a book and share my story in hopes that it would inspire others to lead with love, persevere, and finish strong. My dad, Ellsworth W. Hutchinson Jr., (affectionately known as "Hutch"), has since passed away. He was my hero, the first love of my life, and a proud World War II Army veteran.

Writing and publishing the book has resulted in thousands being encouraged by the nuggets of wisdom found in its pages. This has led to hundreds of speaking engagements over the years to share my story further, and I've motivated many others to tell their stories as well. I am so gratified when I Iearn of newly published authors who were inspired to write their own stories after reading mine. To this day, readers contact me to share the positive impact *3 Slow Nickles* had, and continues to have, on their lives and personal journeys.

And it was all because of Hutch, who believed I had a message to share with a larger audience and insisted I do it.

Initially I reasoned that I did not have time to write this book because I was too busy with my work as a senior executive, community involvements, and commitments as a wife and mother. Well, if you knew my dad, you would quickly come to know that he was the ultimate salesman and did NOT accept "no" for an answer. He reframed my objection as a "not now," and then he let the topic rest—for the moment. Of course, the next time we talked, and every time thereafter, I was met with, "When are you going to write that book? I know there's a book inside of you!" He later told me that he knew deep down I would eventually oblige.

As would happen, in 2015, my amazing daughter, Danielle Watson, was launching her nonprofit with her husband, Dion Watson, to help at-risk youth in Compton, CA. They needed help. Knowing the long-lasting impact that my parents' efforts with social change had in my southeast D.C. neighborhood of Anacostia, I was totally drawn to their cause. I didn't think I could provide the level of support their nonprofit needed while still working full-time. As you'll read in the book, I took a leap of faith and left my job of 25 years, to do two things:

1. Write *3 Slow Nickles*
2. Help Danielle and Dion launch their nonprofit, Discover.YOU Compton

On my dad's 88th birthday, the year following my mom's passing, the book was complete, printed, and in his hands. The smile on his face and pride beaming from his eyes still sits with me today. I did it! I told my story in book form. I made Hutch proud once again!

He couldn't wait to jump in and start reading it. Within 90 minutes, he had finished the book and then, as was our custom, we pulled out the card table and played our favorite game, spades. While I can't remember who won that night, I'm sure if he were still here, he would, with full confidence and without any hesitation, say that he won. For the 10th anniversary edition, I knew from the beginning that Hutch had to be on the cover with me. It's only right, and it's just another way for me to honor him as he rests peacefully.

Hutch transitioned to the stars in March 2024 at nearly 97 years young! He was ready to rejoin his wife, son, brother, parents, and other family who preceded him in death. In complete Hutch fashion, as the consummate gentleman and most selfless human I've ever known, he gave us two months' warning that he would be leaving us. He often shared without fear or trepidation that he was ready to "go up yonder." After our 2024 Friday night card games, I would provide turndown service by getting my dad's room ready with his preferred PJs laid out and helping him take off the awful compression socks he hated. Just before I would tuck him in, he would say with the BIGGEST smile and softest tone, "I think I'm going up yonder tonight, but if I don't, I'll see you tomorrow. I love you, Victoria."

Deep down inside, I knew he was serious. Fighting back tears, I would smile and say, "Oh, Hutch, I'll definitely see you tomorrow!" I later found out that in January 2024, during his last visit to see my middle brother and his family in Tampa, Fla., he told my niece, Lauren, that the trip would certainly be his last. She wasn't quite sure what he meant when he said it, but we came to understand that he was simply putting us all on notice. In late February 2024, he developed a urinary tract infection, a situation that can be very dangerous for seniors. He was admitted to the hospital for a few days and eventually returned home, where my middle sister and BFF, Dana Hutchinson, cared for him around the clock, along with his incredible caregiver, Michelle Temoney.

We could all see the toll the hospital stay had on him, as he had previously been very healthy and independent. However, upon arriving home, his legs were still too weak for him to walk. We had to do everything for him, including bathing him. He did not like this. He began feeling like he was a burden and did not like losing his independence. We assured him that it was our honor and great privilege to have this chance to care for him. Over the coming weeks, it appeared that his condition was improving. Still, we set up an in-home hospice to ensure he was cared for and completely comfortable. During his second week home, he had the biggest burst of energy. I was in denial about what was really happening and convinced myself that he was slowly bouncing back. He was doing so well that week that even the hospice nurse was pleased with his progress.

I had been spending the night and sleeping next to him for two weeks at this point. I noted all of the changes in his health and demeanor. However, even though he repeatedly tried to warn us that he was ready, selfishly, we were not.

Two days before he passed, we had a great day. We played spades just like always and a dear family friend stopped by to groom

Dad's beard, which had grown since his hospital discharge. Hutch finally enjoyed a real meal after fussing about not wanting to eat in the days prior. Tuesday was so good that I asked him if he would be okay if I attended an in-person meeting at work the next day. He laughed and joked and eventually said, "Of course, please go to work tomorrow. I'll be just fine." Once again, I convinced myself that things were looking up and hesitantly drove two hours away to attend a meeting in Philadelphia. I had every intention of returning to Hutch later Wednesday night. While driving back to D.C., there was tons of evening construction and traffic. I called my sister to let her know that I was running later than planned. It would be close to 10 p.m. before I would arrive. At that point, Hutch was resting, and my sister suggested I go home, get a good night's rest, and come in the morning. I hadn't slept more than three hours on any given night for the previous two weeks, so the idea was very tempting. It hadn't dawned on me how tired my body was until she mentioned it. Quite honestly, I had come to really enjoy talking to Hutch on and off all night long. He would randomly and sporadically strike up a conversation, sometimes at 2 a.m. He would request a Frank Sinatra playlist, which led to hours of chatting about the good old days.

Reluctantly, I accepted my sister's offer and drove straight home. Something inside of me was telling me to go back to Hutch's house, but I didn't want to disturb his sleep and had plans to return first thing in the morning to make breakfast and offer relief to Dana and Michelle. But it wasn't meant to be. My phone rang around 4:15 a.m., and my husband Troy answered the phone. All I could hear was Dana screaming. Instantly, my heart dropped into my stomach, and without her saying anything, I knew. I didn't say one word. I calmly got out of bed, washed my face, brushed my teeth, made up my bed, got dressed, and we drove to the house. I was completely numb and muted until I saw him peacefully lying in the bed. Tears rushed down my face, and I allowed guilt to take over. I started screaming that I should have been there, that I should have driven straight to his house, that I should never have left for the meeting. Within minutes, my sister gently reminded me that he didn't want us to see him take his last breath and wanted us to remember him as we last saw him, laughing, talking, eating, and playing cards. God knew her words would immediately provide peace, knowing he had peacefully transitioned to the heavenly stars and had been met by the angels he had been talking to for the last few nights.

And per usual, I jumped into action, just as I had watched him and my mom do my entire life. I bathed him one last time. I lotioned his skin, fully dressed him, and put his favorite WWII Army hat on. I ensured he was well dressed before the undertaker arrived. Even though he wished to be cremated, my dad was very particular about being well-dressed and presentable at all times. Even in those final moments before his body was carefully and gently removed from the home, it was essential that everything was done in honor of this gentle giant and world treasure, the rock of our family.

A few weeks later, in lieu of the funeral he had told us he did NOT want, we threw a party in his honor at his cherished social hub, the Army Navy Country Club in Arlington, VA. We had his favorite homegrown D.C. jazz artist, Marcus Johnson, play and help us celebrate. We retired his Washington Nats and Redskins jerseys. The military presented the flag in a fantastic ceremony, including Whitney Houston's rendition of T*he Star Spangled Banner*. We sang *Take Me Out to the Ball Game*, told stories, and overall had a party that he would have loved. I know he was proud.

The 10 years since the book was first published brought many changes in my personal life as well. Troy, my incredible hubby of 34 years, and I are proud grandparents to King, 9, and Zenzi, 8. We recently celebrated our daughter's 10th wedding anniversary! Troy is now retired after 38 years at Washington Gas Light Company. I've returned to the corporate world and am totally in love with my current position as Executive Vice President and Chief Customer Experience Officer at Tech Network Inc., where I have the much-needed flexibility of being in L.A. with my grandbabies half of the month and back in D.C. with Troy and other family members the other half, when I'm not traveling for work.

In the past decade, the business world has also evolved, especially during the pandemic years. Business was more competitive and more demanding. Now more than ever, it requires a growth mindset. The pandemic years taught us how to be more flexible, adaptable, and agile. It taught us how to be more creative and resourceful, and it showed us just how much we relied on technology to learn, work, and even see loved ones. While I hope we never again have to experience anything as extreme as the world shutting down, I do hope that from the pandemic years, we learned to keep a heart of service, the desire to help others, and the resolve to win, no matter what adversity comes our way.

I am happy to report that though much has changed over the years, the business principles and wisdom I shared in these pages years ago still apply today. The encouragement to drop the guilt and simply commit to doing your best every day is still relevant.

If you're new to my story, welcome! Enjoy the quick, easy read, and remember the best is yet to come! Thank you for being on this journey with me.

Looking forward to the next 10 years. Let's recommit to finishing strong.

Victoria Boston
January 2025

Introduction
to the First Edition

Photo: My parents and I at my brother's funeral. Hutchinson's were built for tough times...

How do you navigate a successful, rising career while maintaining a happy and stable personal life?

Every success story is filled with failures, disappointments, challenges, tears, sweat, and possibly even blood along the way. I intend to take you on a journey and share the lessons learned, pitfalls I avoided and crises overcome. Based on my humble beginnings, I never dreamed I could be a successful corporate professional, involved mom and wife, community volunteer and at times, even a committed full-time college student.

I started out in an entry-level position and ascended to a senior leader in a major corporation and learned along the way, sometimes by trial and error, how to balance my personal and professional life while staying true to my beliefs about what's important.

Think of this book as a series of personal mentoring sessions where you learn from my mistakes and successes and you leave with valuable nuggets of wisdom that you can take and apply to your own situation.

I grew up being mentored by my parents. I didn't realize it at the time, of course, but in retrospect, I see that my home environment was nothing short of an incubator for success — a breeding ground for excellence. To be perfectly honest, not only did I not realize it at the time, I didn't always value it, appreciate it or embrace it. In this book, I pass on the wisdom that shaped me and the experiences and the mindset that resulted in my success.

I am the youngest of seven children and I watched my parents raise us in a small three bedroom house with one bathroom in one of the toughest, poverty-stricken neighborhoods in southeast Washington, DC — Anacostia. My parents taught us resilience and perseverance through adversity. As I watched my parents do what I perceived as the impossible, I learned the mindset of a champion. In fact, I learned that success is always on the other side of adversity when you refuse to quit or give up!

My parents buried one of my sisters, who died not long after birth, and my precious eight-year-old brother, after he was hit by a car on his way home from the playground. Though I was just three years old, I remember the strength they exuded during this stressful time in our lives. It impacted our entire community. They made an intentional decision that, rather than climbing into the caskets and dying with their children, they would live for them instead.

My parents worked every day and showed us first-hand what a real work ethic looked like. Their philosophy was if they didn't work hard, we didn't eat. As you can imagine, there were several mouths to feed including our dog, Fred (who was incredibly greedy) and cat, Morris who really looked like and was named afterthe one in 9Lives brand cat food commercials back in the day! I can't ever remember my parents calling out sick for work or finding a reason to side-step any obligation. If they did, it was a rare occasion. They taught us at an early age that credibility matters — say what you mean and do exactly what you committed to doing. No excuses. I seldom witnessed my parents allow their race or gender to discourage them from being their very best self, although I'm sure it did at times. They seemingly gave their all regardless of endeavor and encouraged us to do the same.

My dad was tops in sales, and the first African American salesman, at a prestigious furniture store. My mom retired as director of research for the Smithsonian's Anacostia Neighborhood Museum in Washington, DC and authored several books during her career. My siblings and I were without excuse. Where we lacked in money, college funds, material possessions, name-brand clothes and fashion, or fancy homes and cars, we never lacked in love, integrity, and hard work. It was in our DNA!

I developed an "it's all good" mindset as a result of experiences growing up as a Hutchinson. Hutchinsons didn't quit, refused to give up, and made a conscious decision to overcome. Hutchinsons played like champions and behaved as winners — period. This mindset didn't mean we wouldn't make dumb mistakes, fall off track, disappoint our parents, siblings or ourselves — because we most certainly did, but what it did mean was that we got up off the canvas, learned the valuable lesson and realized that it's all good, no matter what. As you can imagine, it wasn't always easy to embody this. There were times in all of our lives where we felt like quitting, giving up and forgot that we were champions. We were highly encouraged to push through at every turn.

One of my favorite Nike quotes is: "Greatness has no peak. Willpower knows no obstacles. Quit making excuses, putting it off, complaining about it, dreaming about it, whining about it, crying about it, believing you can't, worrying if you can, waiting until you're older, skinnier, richer, braver, or all around better. Suck it up, hold on tight, say a prayer, make a plan and just do it." Every time I see it, it reminds me that no matter what — it's all good. There will always be a reason to quit, make an excuse, or doubt yourself and those around you. Whenever my mind shifts in this direction, I try to quickly remember that in the end, all things work together for good. Because I truly believe it's all good, I can simply execute the plan and just do it!

Not too long after my mom died, I remember having conversations with my dad and sisters, specifically about the impact she not only had on our lives but on all with whom she came in contact. We talked about her legacy and how we had to continue to live for her and carry on her good work – standing for what's right, encouraging others, giving in to purpose, and making a real difference in the world. It was in one of these uplifting conversations that my dad turned to me and said, "you know Victoria, there is a book inside of you." While most people who know me, call me Vicky, my father has always called me Victoria. "If I wanted to call you Vicky, I would have named you Vicky," he is known to say. He reminded me that my mother authored several books for the Smithsonian – *The Anacostia Story: 1608 to 1930*, *Anna J. Cooper: A Voice from the South* and *Out of Africa: West African Kingdoms to Colonization*, just to name a few. He said to me that if my mother could write such amazing books, full of history and facts untold in the average classroom, yet essential to us knowing who we really are and where we came from, that certainly, I could pause and tell my story.

Now that I have lived a little, experienced a few setbacks, comebacks and level of success that I never imagined possible, I have the opportunity to share with you, in hopes that you too will connect to what's possible and quickly walk in the vocation to which you were called.

When you finish this easy-to-read, power-packed book full of actionable nuggets, my desire is that you will be inspired and equipped to fully engage in your life. Above all else, I want to offer hope. I want you to walk away knowing that there is something good out there just for you.

You can juggle demanding responsibilities successfully. You can be successful in corporate America and stay true to who you are. It CAN be done!

Ready? Let's go…

"Your only limit is you."

– Nike

Take a moment and jot down your perceived obstacles faced and be prepared to tackle them as you take this journey with me.

Rules of Engagement

Photo: #TeamBoston. Troy & Vicky celebrating 25 years of marriage.

As the youngest of seven children growing up in southeast Washington, DC, a neighborhood full of poverty, crime, alarming high-school dropout rates and pockets of hopelessness, I was always clear about the expectations in my household. I like to refer to my childhood home by its street number, 2415. Mom and dad were crystal clear on what behaviors and habits were acceptable at 2415. They were even more explicit on what would not be tolerated as a Hutchinson. The rules of engagement at 2415 were clear then and evident even now in my own household.

One of my parents' non-negotiable rules was that the bed should be made the moment you step out of it. This used to drive me absolutely nutty because I used to think it was pointless to make up a bed that you were going to eventually climb back into. This habit is so embedded in me (no pun intended) that, 40 years later, I'm still doing it. It's such an automatic response when I wake up that I even do it in hotels when I know there is staff compensated to do it for me.

My dad, Ellsworth W. Hutchinson, Jr., was former military and he worked several jobs until he found his true love – sales! In fact, he was the first African-American salesman at the prestigious Curtis Bros. Furniture store in Anacostia where he was #1 in sales year after year. In 1959, the furniture store commissioned Bassett Furniture to build the largest chair imaginable to be displayed in the parking lot of Curtis Bros. on

Martin Luther King Jr. Avenue. in Southeast Washington, D.C. A national historical landmark, it is affectionately known as "The Big Chair" and stands 19.5 feet tall, weighs 4,600 pounds and resembles a dining room chair made of African mahogany wood. George Curtis, the owner of the store, presented my dad with a black onyx ring with four diamonds and a big chair etched in the stone a result of his exceptional sales performance. At the age of 88, my dad still wears that ring today, more than 40 years later. By the way, all of his grandchildren have claimed that ring. What they clearly don't know is that I've already had that conversation with Dad! I guess we will all share and enjoy the coveted ring one day.

Etiquette is golden

My dad went on to excel in furniture sales until retirement and continues to be everyone's resident expert on mattresses. Because of his love of sales and the pure enjoyment of instantly connecting with everyone he comes in contact with, it took three acts of retiring before he finally hung up the jersey at the precious age of 83. I believe this is exactly where I get my natural salesmanship and ability to connect with others! A few of my dad's most critical rules of engagement were and still are:

- Always be on time, in fact be early.
- Always keep your word; never break a promise.
- Be kind to everyone because relationships matter.

As I previously mentioned, my mom was an educator, historian, researcher for the Smithsonian, author and community activist. She was the voice for those without one and always took a stand for what she believed was right for her family and for the community where she lived and served until her passing in the fall of 2014. As I reflect on my childhood, I recall that my mom worked a lot and probably could have done a better job paying attention to her own health. In today's health-conscious environment with fitness centers conveniently located near shopping centers and an overload of information on healthy eating and natural remedies, it seems easier to incorporate a fitness regimen into our modern lives. Unfortunately, that wasn't the case for my mom.

Still, she was very smart and witty with exceptionally high standards for herself and everyone she encountered. Her core belief was that failure was not an option and that regardless of color, class, gender, or economic status, we, her children, had everything we needed to be successful. Excuses of any kind were not accepted in our home as a child and even after we moved and started families of our own, she continued to remind us of this. Of course, we made mistakes, but the use of the word "can't" wasn't entertained or tolerated EVER! She even convinced us that the word "can't" wasn't in the dictionary.

When we did make mistakes, she was right there to encourage us to quickly learn from them. Oddly enough, learning the difference between making mistakes and not making excuses was difficult for me to wrap my head around as a young adult. Seemed like whenever I made a mistake, I had a ton of excuses for why it happened. I think what my mom was trying to teach us was that, even though we are created in the image and likeness of a perfect God, we as humans are far from perfect. Hence mistakes would be made; however, we were expected to learn from them. I grew up being super-competitive, critical of and hard on myself. It wasn't until later in life that I stopped beating myself up when I failed. Like any child, I never wanted to disappoint my parents. I struggled to differentiate between giving my best and sometimes falling short and failing because I simply didn't give it my all. There's a big difference between the two.

A book for idle hands

My parents strongly believed that education was our currency. They wanted us always to keep a book in our hands. But not just any book. They encouraged us to read books that exposed us to ideas, thoughts and places that we may not have yet experienced. While we may not have been thrilled at the onset, the habit of constantly reading certainly added to our curiosity! If we ever grumbled that we were bored, we knew a book was coming directly our way. It's so hard to admit this knowing my mom was an author and had such a love for books, but I actually did not start enjoying books of any kind until I was well into my 20s. As a child and a young adult, reading always felt like a chore. Now, I always keep a book in my hand. What started as a dreaded duty, is now a joy.

In elementary and junior high school particularly, my school principals and teachers were often times my mom's best and closest friends. As a result, the teachers were tougher on us in class. While it may sound great now that my parents, especially my mom, knew almost every educator in the city, it surely didn't seem great then. They all kept a close eye on us. It really didn't seem fair at the time; we had no idea how much of a blessing it was to have such involved parents in our education and school system overall.

The neighborhood where we grew up, and where my dad still resides, was very close knit. The neighbors were well aware of the standards that Louise Daniel Hutchinson set for her children – the Hutchinson Clan. Whether home, at school or playing in the neighborhood, we were consistently held to the highest standard. I can remember a time in the 6th grade when an oversized classmate who was the known bully attempted to take my lunch during recess. At the time, I had a red metal Wonder Woman lunch box with a black shiny handle. (I wish I held on to it because it's going for $250 on eBay today!) Bologna and cheese was my favorite sandwich with chips and a drink. On special occasions like birthdays or when I received exceptional report cards, I looked forward to a Chips Ahoy chocolate chip cookie as an extra treat! On this particular day, the bully approached me on the black top. The black top is where we practiced track after school, but it also doubled as the hang out area during lunch recess when the weather permitted. While I don't remember all the details of the exchange, what I do remember and likely never will forget is having to defend myself after being shoved and told to relinquish my lunch and favorite (and only) lunch box. Rather than cave to her demands, I hit her in the head with my metal lunch box and as a result she required stitches. The incident spread like wildfire at school, home and in the neighborhood.

I can remember receiving multiple lectures from my homeroom teacher, parents, the adults in my neighborhood, and the principal on how violence doesn't solve anything and that I should have alerted an adult at the onset of being picked on instead of taking matters into my own hands. I can especially remember my principal saying, "Hutchinsons don't behave this way." Of course, my oldest sister applauded my efforts and condoned my behavior. She was all about self-defense at all costs! Growing up in a neighborhood like ours, you were constantly playing out in your head how you would defend yourself to and from school as well as when we hung out at the Fort Stanton neighborhood recreation center – now refurbished with a community room named after my mom.

Moms know best

None of the advice on keeping the peace and telling an adult seemed to make sense to me at the time but years later, I found myself giving that same advice to my daughter when she was in the 2nd grade. My daughter's school went from kindergarten through 8th grade, which meant she rode the school bus with children up to 14-years-old. I can still hear myself saying, "Remember, Danielle, if anyone bothers you on the bus, let the bus driver know." But in the back of my mind, I was thinking how I stopped that bully in her tracks handling things my way.

In hindsight, my mom knew best. She knew the potentially devastating effects of allowing our environment to define us. Poor choices in friends could derail us. Allowing the streets to be our teacher could literally kill our purpose and potential, if not our mortal bodies. Many of mom's words of wisdom reverberate even now, especially these nuggets:

- Reading is not optional; lifelong learning is a requirement.
- Never quit, never give up.
- Know who you are, know that you are loved, and live out your purpose.

The Hutchinson rules of engagement absolutely helped shaped me into the disciplined person that I am today. As you reflect on your life and upbringing, what are the things that shaped who you are? What are the values that you live by?

Good fences

It's vitally important to establish the rules for your home and family, even if your family only consists of one member — you! There will always be competing interests, and it is essential that you establish these principles before problems crop up.

Author, Teri Johnson, a licensed mental health counselor with a masters in psychology, has written extensively about relationships and suggests that success in marriage comes from identifying, clearly articulating and executing boundaries, or what I call rules of engagement. Boundaries are viewed as fences around our homes and those boundaries inform those governed by them, she says. The boundaries help others around us know what's expected if they choose to come inside the fences of our lives. Establishing the rules of engagement is a constant work in progress, says Johnson. As with anything, there are seasons in our lives — marriages, starting a family, buying a home, careers, and the aging process. Thus, the rules may be fluid and dynamic versus static.

As I transitioned from my childhood home at 2415 to my own home, 6010, I too wanted to ensure that there were clear rules of engagement, established for my own home and family. My husband always had high standards for himself and when I became Mrs. Troy P. Boston, we wanted the Boston family to live by a certain creed:

- Bostons are strong.
- Bostons don't quit.

- Bostons finish what they start.
- Bostons are credible.
- Above all else, Bostons put God and family first.

Regardless of my position, title or responsibility at work or in the community, nothing and no one came before the Boston clan at 6010. That was the goal, anyway, to put family before career, and sometimes I hit that goal and sometimes not so much.

Looking back, I can see that the rules of the house that my husband and I created — rules we created based on what was really important to us – kept us grounded and centered. We never really wrote the rules down or posted them around the house. We discussed them as a family in casual settings, lived them out, modeled the behavior and challenged one another when we veered off course. It seemingly became second nature, our unwritten standard operating procedures.

For example, one of my favorite rules was not going to bed angry (easier said than done). Even if we were angry with someone outside of our household, we encouraged each other to resolve whatever issue we had. As we liked to say, "squash the beef" before bedtime so as to not carry today's drama into tomorrow.

Family before career

Before making any decisions regarding a new position, career move, promotion, relocation opportunity, new responsibilities at work, or volunteering in my community, I would weigh the impact it would have on my home life.

I strived to make every decision with 6010 in mind. Yet, I remember a time when I made the decision to live apart from my family to accept a job hundreds of miles away, one that likely would have been catastrophic for my family relationships. I frequently discussed my career mobility with my husband, or at least I thought I was having what I considered frequent conversations. I worked for a national firm where employee relocations from state to state happened all the time.

However, this near-miss happened when I failed to consider everything that was going on, not only in our immediate home but with our parents and grandparents. It's funny how when you really want something, you can justify anything! This was the case when I was twice offered a promotion by a very senior leader who had a reputation as one you really wanted to work for if you aspired to attain career mobility and growth. The first time the promotion was offered, I declined it because of bad timing and now the question was back on the table. The only real dilemma for me was that the job was in Tampa, Florida, at the time. While mobility was a topic often discussed at home, there was something that I hadn't fully factored into the situation: my mom and my mother-in-law's health had both begun to decline. In a selfish moment, I was able to initially sell my husband on the idea that this was a great opportunity and one that I shouldn't pass up again. After all, I had worked hard and deserved it, or at least that is what I told myself. Being the salesperson that I am, I convinced everyone that this was a great idea!

Troy and I had decided that for this particular opportunity, if I accepted the promotion, I would move down to Tampa alone and commute back to the DC area a few times a month. He and Danielle would stay back to avoid disrupting her schooling and his career. I really wanted this promotion and even more so the chance to work for a dynamic leader.

To complicate matters, I had some so-called mentors whispering in my ear, "Vicky, if you turn this down, they will NEVER offer you another promotion. You would be crazy NOT to take this." I was afraid that refusing the promotion a second time would mean lights out – career suicide.

As you can imagine, I had a huge decision to make. Although, I seemingly had the support of my husband (not so much from our daughter), something just wasn't sitting right with me. However, I accepted the promotion. Within 24 hours, it hit me that my decision was all wrong. How could I leave my husband, who is an only child, to care for his sick mother, care for our teenaged daughter and help my siblings with my ailing mother, while I was hundreds of miles away?

We all knew that every time I got a new position, I would dive in full bore the first 90 days to get my arms around it. The idea that I would bounce back and forth between DC and Tampa was neither reasonable nor realistic. But the wheels for my relocation were in motion. In my mind, it would most certainly mean career suicide to have a change of heart and turn it down at this point. It was only when I remembered one of the Boston family's core values, God and family first, that sanity and serenity returned. Looking back, I have no doubt that moving to Tampa at that time would have been catastrophic for my family. It would have been undue stress on Troy, which would have no doubt put a heavy strain on our marriage. Not long after, my mother-in-law passed. I am eternally grateful that I was where I was supposed to be at the time my family needed me.

As it turned out, this critical decision wasn't career suicide after all. I received promotions thereafter. In fact, this wasn't the last time I turned down a great opportunity due to poor timing for my family. A few years later, I had the chance to take an assignment in Basking Ridge, New Jersey, near my company's headquarters. The position, while not a promotion, was a lateral move that would have positioned me for tremendous visibility by the chairman. The way the team was set up back then, this position reported to a vice president who answered to a senior vice president who reported directly to the chairman. Having gained some wisdom and strength from the previous experiences, I was able to really think it all through, discuss it with Troy, Danielle and other close family and friends. In the end, while everything looked great on paper, especially as it related to career upward mobility, it came down to what was the best decision for 6010 overall. Without any hesitation or ambiguity, I thanked the leaders for the consideration and job offer, explained my family situation which included my mom's further and rapid health decline, and respectfully turned down the position.

Consider the costs

Think it through, remembering your established rules of

engagement, and consider the cost of the decision as well as the long-lasting consequences!

Don't wait until a job offer or other life-altering opportunity presents itself to initiate or have "the conversation." Talk to your spouse, close family, and/or significant other regarding life-altering opportunities that can cause shock waves throughout your home and personal life. Oftentimes, the shock waves come because you haven't discussed things that could happen before they happen. The benefit and advantage of having "the conversation" ahead of time is to avoid the surprises and not to catch anyone off guard. This can be very problematic on all fronts. When you're not sure about your mobility, ability to relocate the family and/or ability to travel, it can cause you to waffle in your decision-making at work and at home. It can also cause you to be viewed as indecisive by the person offering you the opportunity. Knowing in advance if you're able to relocate your family, with or without restrictions, and if you are able to travel, whether with limited or advance notice, is super important. It was my goal to have "the conversation" quarterly or as often as needed to avoid surprises. I also kept my leadership team informed so they were just as clear on my status and limitations, if any existed. Once you are crystal clear about your "6010," the rules of engagement and boundaries for your home life, you can be clear with everyone else. Clearly set expectations.

Have the conversation

While we may not have always nailed all the rules at 6010, the

Bostons set some lofty goals:

- Put nothing before God and family — period.
- Ask and know what is important to each other and seek to support it; whatever "it" is.
- Make decisions as a family and consider the impact on 6010.
- Be on time and keep your word. Commitments matter.
- Communicate, communicate, and communicate some more – NO secrets!
- Be willing to sacrifice for the greater good.
- Embody the Team Boston mindset – we all have on the same jersey.

Dwight D. Eisenhower said, "We succeed only as we identify in life, or in war, or in anything else, a single overriding objective and make all other considerations bend to that one objective." One of my mentors, Jonathan Sprinkles, often says it this way – "know what bows to what and know what is absolutely first and then second." What is your one objective that you will ensure everything else bends or bows to support it?

Take a moment and consider the following questions to help you define and support your "6010."

What's most important to my family?

....

....

....

....

....

....

2. What are our family goals?

....

....

....

....

....

....

3. Am I making decisions today to help us achieve the family goal(s)?

....

....

....

....

....

....

....

4. Have I had "the conversation" with my family, loved ones and those in my support system about mobility and the ability to travel for work? Yes/No

a. Am I mobile?

....

....

b. What are my limitations (i.e. Can I relocate the family domestically but not internationally, East Coast only, etc.)

....

....

....

....

....

c. If I am not mobile now, when will I be?

....

....

....

....

....

....

d. Can I travel with limited to no advanced notice and ensure family support is in place?

....

....

e. If able to travel, is it limited to 25%, 50% or 75%? Do I have the infrastructure in place to support a job with 100% travel requirements?

....

....

....

....

5. As it relates to relocating and/or travel, what are the deal breakers for my "6010"?

....

....

....

....

....

....

....

....

If it's been a while since you've had "the conversation" or perhaps you've never had this talk with your family, significant other, loved ones and those in support, today is a great day to get "the conversation" started. It's up to you to ensure your "6010" is set up for success, provided for and protected at all costs.

Make a date to get "the conversation" started.

"Never apologize for having high standards. People who really want to be in your life will rise up to meet them."

– Unknown

Drop the Guilt

Photo: January 1, 2015 - A mother's kiss before her daughter's wedding. Being there when it matters most...

My daughter, Danielle, is a very successful and productive adult, now happily married. She graduated from Pepperdine University in three years with a bachelor's degree in communication, marketing and advertising. She and her husband, Dion, are professional dancers, choreographers and actors who run a nonprofit organization serving underprivileged youth in Compton, the hard-scrabble Los Angeles suburb known for gangsta rap where Dion was born and raised. At such young ages, Danielle and Dion have traveled the world and toured with some of the biggest names in the entertainment industry, including Beyonce, Mariah Carey, Will.i.am, Usher, and many more. Their passion to give back to their community is the motivation for the great work they are embarking on today. I beam with pride at the daughter my husband and I raised. To see the accomplished, compassionate woman she has become puts everything into perspective. If I had any doubt before about whether or not I was at home enough, those questions don't loom as large in my mind anymore. I gave her the very best pieces of me — Boston family values and ethics and an abundance of nurturing and love, and I think her life reflects that. So if you were to ask Danielle was I home when she lost her first tooth, chances are she wouldn't remember and as she nears age 27, she likely doesn't care.

But you couldn't convince me of that when I was working late one evening to prepare for a big meeting the following day, and I got "the call" from hubby that her first tooth had fallen out!

OMG, I was guilt-ridden and thought I was going straight to hell that moment for missing such a major milestone in my one-and-only child's life.

This wasn't the first time I was overwhelmed with guilt and wouldn't be the last. How about the time I missed her dance recital in the 7th grade when she had a solo and huge part in the production? Or the time when she wanted both mom and dad to accompany her class on the pumpkin patch field trip? Then, there was the basketball game when she was the starting point guard and, of course, with so much always going on, I had the location of the gym wrong and missed half if not almost the entire game!

I really thought life was over when my flight was delayed out of the dreaded Newark, New Jersey, airport and I missed my daughter's 12th birthday. Every birthday is a big, darn deal in our house, only because I always tried to make it so. But this was the BIG 12th birthday! Troy and I had made plans to take her to dinner to celebrate being on the verge of teendom, but due to circumstances beyond my control I would not be able to make her birthday. Seriously, was the world really coming to an end? Of course not, but I had worked myself up and had actually convinced myself that I was the worst mom in the whole wide world for missing such a special day, as if it couldn't be celebrated or acknowledged at some other point in time. It's so cool that I can actually laugh at this today, but at the time, there was so much unnecessary drama!

I was frantic when I realized that there was no way that I was going to get home in time for her birthday dinner. Very calmly, my husband said, "No worries, I will just pick up Charnee' (her best friend at the time) and take them to Dannie's favorite restaurant. It will work out fine." Finally, it hit me to drop the self-imposed guilt and redirect the negative energy consuming me and focus only on what I could control. I contacted Troy and asked him to have the waiter bring dessert to the table after dinner and call me so I could sing happy birthday by cell phone. Of course, this was long before Skype and FaceTime. My husband wasn't actually thrilled about this idea because he knew I was making this way bigger than it needed to be. My daughter understood when he explained the flight delays and was happy her best friend was able to join her on a school night. Even though both Troy and Danielle understood and didn't express any disappointment, I couldn't help but feel like I let them down.

After several experiences like this, I decided to ask my daughter, who was very active in extra-curricular activities and sports, what events and activities were most important to her. I also asked my husband, who volunteered weekly at our local church and coached boys basketball, what events and activities were most important to him. He was extremely supportive of my career and I wanted to be sure I was making every effort to support what was also important to him. This one conversation changed everything! Activities that I had elevated to high-priority status, in some cases were lower on the totem pole, and other things they were involved in that seemed less significant in my mind ended up being a big deal to them. The process of talking this through, actually taking the time to flush it all out, alleviated so much stress. It felt like it added ten years back to my life.

For the critical dates and events that they identified like the spring dance recital with a solo role or the basketball game that determined if the team advanced to the playoffs, I moved heaven and earth to be there. For those games, track meets, field trips, and dance recitals I could attend as well as those I could not, I ensured there was always an army of fans and full-blown cheering section made up of family, friends, and neighbors who loudly chanted "go Boston" and supported the cause!

Being strategic, asking what was important to them, and taking the necessary steps to make it happen, made all the difference. Here's the deal, even if I fell short from time to time (and believe me, I did) and was unable to make all the family events and activities deemed important, they appreciated the fact that I tried everything in my power to make it happen. Obviously, I still missed some critical dates but my network of supporters and extended family certainly helped to make up for my absence.

The everything calendar

One of the big lessons here was to put pride aside and ask for help. I found that too many times, I was trying to make it all happen and nearly killing myself in the process. At other times, I was simply moving too fast and forgetting to add critical dates to the calendar, which caused unnecessary confusion. This taught me to slow down a bit and take time out every Sunday to do a calendar review as a family to ensure that we were all on the same page. Sometimes, there were just too many moving parts to memorize who's on first base and who's on second! To this day, I put everything on the calendar and couldn't manage life without it. Forget having a separate personal and business calendar; that quickly became way too complicated. One calendar with everything – doctor appointments, back-to-school meetings, dance rehearsals, birthdays, anniversaries, big meetings at work and more. You get the point. EVERYTHING goes on the calendar. If it wasn't in writing, it probably would not get done.

Another lesson learned was remembering to explain "why" I would miss an important event to help ease the disappointment. If I knew I was not going to be able to make a dance recital, school play, family dinner or anything important to our family, I would explain the scheduling conflict in advance, especially to my daughter, and would reassure her of the support that would be there. She quickly understood when I took the time to break it all down, although hardly ever pleased (understandably so). Every blue moon, she would ask why I had to be the one who had to fly here and there to meet with a customer or why I had to work late to fix a problem. Truthfully, I didn't expect her to always get it. Heck, sometimes, I asked myself those same questions! Why me?

There were some field trips that she really wanted me to chaperone, and others weren't such a big deal at all. With limited vacation days each year, and having a very demanding job that required tons of travel, negotiating became a regular occurrence at 6010! One of the strategies I quickly embraced was measuring out vacation according to school activities.

My annual leave was mostly eaten up by the school calendar, so we tried to schedule our family vacations around spring break each year as well as bank a few vacation days for the unexpected. With Troy and I both working for utility companies, they seldom closed for inclement weather. In fact, our companies really didn't close for anything. As a result, we required a long list of backup supporters that we could call on in a pinch for school and family emergencies in case one or both of us couldn't make it.

I am very grateful for the unconditional love and support Troy provided during my career journey. We didn't really sit down at any point during our careers and plot out who would go after the promotion or whose career would need to take a back seat. We were very fortunate that our career paths complimented each other and overall supported the needs of the family. For many years, Troy worked out in the field as a senior technician for Washington Gas, a local utility company. He loved his flexible schedule which allowed him to make schedule changes as needed when I was away on business travel. Thankfully, Danielle was never a latchkey child. It was important to us to have one or both parents at home in the evening after s chool to assist with homework and to prepare dinner. Later in our careers as we both progressed, we discussed the opportunities and the impact on our family. Fortunately, the promotions Troy accepted still allowed him to pick up much of the slack at home, such as preparing dinner, ensuring Danielle made it to evening dance rehearsals, keeping the house clean, laundry and so much more. Troy successfully led and continues to lead a great group of technicians and staff supervisors and is responsible for the gas pressure for his territory in Prince George's County, Maryland, minutes outside of Washington, DC. We always approached our marriage and family responsibilities as a partnership and I can honestly say, it was nearly an automatic response when one of us needed to step up in a bigger way to support the other.

Vince Lombardi said, "Once you agree upon the price you and your family must pay for success, it enables you to ignore the minor hurts, the opponent's pressure and the temporary failures." I couldn't agree more, and it was most liberating the day I learned to drop the guilt!

Quality time matters

Go through the steps of asking your loved ones what's important to them and understand what's important to you as well. You just might find that what you suspected was a big deal to your family and friends, may not be after all. Because I traveled most weeks for work, I made a concerted effort to visit my parents on Sundays. I would get so frustrated with myself if I couldn't spend the entire afternoon with them because I assumed, without asking, that's what they wanted. One Sunday afternoon when I was visiting with my parents, an issue arose at work. I was on a call in an attempt to get the situation resolved and after hanging up the phone, my mom said in a very kind yet sarcastic voice, "When you're in my house visiting, stay off your cell." In other words, she wanted me in the moment with her even if the moments were short. I learned really quickly that it wasn't the duration of my visit that mattered at all but ensuring the time was well spent and meaningful. Who knew? Prior to that encounter, I had never asked either mom or dad what was truly important to them when I visited.

The "so what" of all of this: Stop wasting energy on guilt. Take a moment and just find out what's important to those you care about and those who care about you. What are you feeling guilty about today? I challenge you to journal it below. After you get it on paper, whatever it is, I now challenge you to simply let it go!

"You were put on this earth to achieve your greatest self, to live out your purpose, and to do it courageously."

– Dr. Steve Maraboli

Finding Balance

Photo: My great-nephew, Caden, catching his balance! You really can have it all... perhaps, just not all at the same time.

While attending a women's leadership conference several years ago in San Francisco, one of the panelists really stood out to me. This speaker was of special interest to me because at that time she was CEO of the Oakland Raiders, the first and only female "C" level executive in the male-dominated NFL. Her name is Amy Trask. She retired from this position back in 2013, not too long after I had the pleasure of hearing her speak. Her golden nuggets and overall remarks at the conference have stayed with me and I refer back to them often. I can remember the question-answer part of the panel discussion so vividly, especially the infamous question about how to balance work and home life (which seems to come up at nearly every conference I attend). I remember someone asking Amy specifically, how someone in her position, with so much responsibility, visibility and history in the making, balance work, home, community, fun, personal development, and of course the "S" word - sleep. I recall her simple yet profound response that made such a big difference in my life and in the way I viewed my own work-home life balance (or should I say, my struggle with the perfect balance).

Amy responded that she clearly communicated to her family, friends and loved ones that during football season, all bets were off. My interpretation of her comments was that she was upfront about her demanding work schedule and what her family and others who depended on her could count on during the season. I also remembered her sharing how she intentionally made herself super available during the off season and that, in fact, was her balance. I realized in that moment, that we all have to figure out our own balance equation. What works for one working mom, dad, or family, may not work for others. When my husband and I decided early on to define what "6010" meant to us, it was an attempt to strike a healthy balance in our home life.

Depending on the seasons in our life, some things that used to be deal breakers, like eating together as a family when my daughter was much younger, did not hold the same weight when she was in high school and had a crazy school and extracurricular schedule. As I reflect back to the early days of my marriage to 25 years later, one of our non-negotiables that remains in place today is worshiping together as a family at our local church. Now that my daughter is grown, married and living clear across the country, whenever she and our son-in-law come home to visit, they, too, look forward to attending Sunday morning service with us. This is one that has always been super-important to us and has sustained us as a family.

Tackling defeat

I had Danielle when I was 19, right out of high school. Needless to say, that made it a little challenging to attend college full time. I tried to take a few classes here and there and failed miserably. At the time, I wasn't organized enough nor mature enough to balance all of that simultaneously. I can remember one of the counselors at my community college saying to me that I was simply wasting money since I had only passed maybe two out of eight classes. I felt defeated and quit on the spot. I had bouts of starting and stopping and always had a great excuse for quitting. Wow, the more I think about it, I had actually perfected the art of quitting. At least, I had convinced myself that the excuses were good reasoning. When my daughter was in the 6th grade, her teacher asked her to memorize a poem and share it with the classroom. Here's an excerpt from it:

"Excuses are tools of the incompetent which create
monuments of nothingness.

Those who specialize in them
are seldom good in anything…"
—*Author Unknown*

There are many versions of this poem; however, these are the lines that I clearly remember Danielle repeating around the house over and over until memorization set in. I'm not sure what triggered the teacher to share this poem, but, I believe it wasn't by happenstance that my child was charged with learning it. To this day, I believe that poem was for me. It was in those moments that I was very comfortable with my ongoing excuses to quit school and had no regret. The words in this poem challenged my complacency.

Even though the poem had a profound impact on my life, I didn't make changes in my life instantly. As you can imagine, I started and stopped a few more times before I actually wholeheartedly embraced college. I had a colleague, Charles Casteel, who started at the company around the same time I did, and our paths sort of tracked together as we progressed from our jobs as customer service representatives. By that time, I had jumped from an entry-level position to customer service to the director of several call centers with responsibility for more than 2,000 customer service representatives across nine states. One day, my coworker Charles said very casually, "Vic, you've stopped and started school so many times, if you had just taken one course each semester over these past 10 years, you would have had three degrees by now!" And guess what? He wasn't exaggerating. It really had been 10 years off and on. Ouch, that hurt then and I can remember feeling inwardly deflated. I certainly wasn't going to show an outward expression to affirm his comment. I had too much pride and attitude for that. Why couldn't he have used Zig Ziglar's encouraging words? "Put all excuses aside and remember this: YOU are capable." Geez!

Finally, one day while attending choir rehearsal at church, choir director Kathy Horry informed us that she would be graduating from the University of Maryland online program, UMUC. That was a new concept to me. Up until this point, all my on and off studies were on campus, sitting in a classroom with a professor lecturing in the front. Embarrassed that all these years later, I still didn't have my degree, I didn't join in the conversation about Kathy. I may have congratulated her, as I was sincerely happy about her accomplishment but I absolutely didn't want to get caught in a conversation about completing my degree.

Kathy must have picked up on the vibe and sure enough, she asked me when I would be done with school as she knew I had taken classes in years past. I was ready with my canned excuse. I didn't have time with my demanding schedule, job responsibilities, heavy travel and caring for a husband and daughter. I figured, a degree just wasn't in the cards. In 30 seconds flat, she had the solution! Online learning was really starting to become very popular and by this time, students could actually complete their entire degree online.

I shot off another excuse that my learning style was to be sitting in a classroom on the front row, directly up under the teacher. I had convinced myself that I couldn't learn any other way. I explained to Kathy that if I got a "D" or lower that I would have to pay the company back. I shared with her that there was no way I could take a class online and actually pass it. Oh yeah, did I mention that my company paid for our schooling up to $8,000 annually? Actually, years prior when I was wasting time stopping and starting, it was unlimited tuition assistance. My company paid for the classes in advance and employees never had to come out of pocket unless we received the "D" letter grade or failed altogether. What in the world was I thinking??? Kathy ever so kindly encouraged me to sign up for the fall semester. She was on to all of my excuses, and she removed them. She said that if, for some strange reason, I received a "D" or failed, which she had no reason to believe that I would, she would pay my company back. My classes were $1500 each. This wasn't chump change; this was adult money.

Now what? I was without excuse. Recalling the words of the poem and the expression on Danielle's face as she recited it around the house, I enrolled in Strayer University's online program without hesitation hoping to secure a bachelor's degree in business administration. This would certainly require some serious work-home-life balance given that I was married, mother of a teenager who happened to have her own crazy schedule between school, dance, basketball, and track! Part of the registration process was providing the transcript from my community college. I can remember going to the school, requesting it, paying for it, and laughing at myself the entire drive from the community college to the Strayer campus in Camp Springs, Maryland. Essentially, it was nearly pointless to get the transcript. I was starting from scratch. I think I was able to transfer no more than two classes worth of credits. The only class I didn't have to take at Strayer while getting my undergrad was accounting.

Lessons from the sidelines

Key lesson: Make every minute count, nothing's promised. While you don't need to strike the perfect balance; having some semblance of it is key.

I took up Amy Trask's game plan for finding the balance that worked for "6010" while I was pursuing my degree. While I was working on my bachelor's and subsequently MBA degree, all bets were off. Even before enrolling in school, I solicited the support of my husband, daughter, and other close family and friends, as it truly takes a village to keep all the balls in the air. With my demanding work schedule and constant travel, I knew I couldn't walk this journey alone. There were times that I may have needed my sisters to cook dinner for us, be at the house when the plumber arrived for repairs or even run to school and pick up Danielle when she was ill because I just couldn't do it all, all at once. I needed the full support of everyone around me. I wanted to be sure that before I made such a huge personal and financial commitment, that my immediate family and responsibilities at work would not suffer. Once I got the green light from all involved, it was full steam ahead.

My discretionary time was slim to none. I can recall Sunday family dinners, most often hosted at my home, and while tons of laughter and fun were being had by all downstairs in the kitchen and family room, I was locked up in my office upstairs cranking out papers for three and sometimes four classes at a time. I will admit, four classes per semester as a full-time mom, wife, employee, community volunteer, not to mention non-stop travel for work was a bit insane, but I did what I had to do.

I will be the first to admit that this was not an easy process or journey. There were times when my daughter needed help as she was taking advanced courses in high school and I was trying to get my homework done. For a few semesters, probably more than I would care to admit, my family lived off cereal for dinner during the week and I was thrilled if I got more than four hours of sleep. The lack of sleep probably had a negative impact on me physically and emotionally. But I made a conscious effort to put on my game face at work. Although I hate to admit it, I took my family for granted at times and they experienced my crankiness more than anyone else. Depending on the travel schedule at work and school demands, there were days when I'm sure Troy and Danielle wished they didn't speak to me at all since I wasn't always too nice. I am truly grateful that, for the most part, they didn't take it personal and knew I needed sleep and even on some occasions, food. I'm sure it wasn't funny then, but we certainly can laugh about it now that it's behind us. At times I didn't realize just how cranky I had become and they would dish it right back. And I would be the one with an attitude for having to put up with two cranks! Some nerve I had.

My last two semesters during my undergrad studies were the absolute worst. For some crazy reason, I thought it would be brilliant to take economics, logic, and math all at once. Surely, they all fit together so it would be like taking one big class, right? Absolutely not. A few weeks in, I was drowning, not eating, not sleeping and secretly crying crocodile tears whenever I was alone. I had too much pride to cry in front of anyone about school. One day, my middle sister, Dana, called and heard it in my voice. I think I actually had a meltdown on the phone and told her that I was calling up the school to quit. Who needs a degree anyway? I've worked hard and excelled to executive status without my bachelors degree, so why should I torture myself and neglect my family? At least in that vulnerable moment, that's how I saw it.

Being the great listener and most compassionate person on earth, she said, "Earth to Victoria, have you lost your mind! You are too close to quit. You will NOT quit. Hang up this phone, call the school ASAP and get a tutor. Do you hear me?"

Back in the game

Tears streaming down my face, I barely got out the word, "Yep."

I hung up the phone, still crying, even more dramatic now than when I was speaking to Dana, called Strayer and asked for a tutor. Within 24 hours, one was assigned and within 3 days, I was receiving tutoring from a professor on the Camp Springs campus.

I still couldn't make too much sense of economics, so on top of the school's tutor, I asked one of the kindest and smartest colleagues in finance, Jeff Gold, to help me and he did. (And even when Danielle was at Pepperdine University, enrolled in economics as a sophomore, she too struggled and the one and only Jeff Gold tutored her by phone all the way from Maryland. She got a "B.") Believe it or not, I did muster up the courage to finish and was more determined than ever to pass those classes. I ended up with a "B" in logic, an "A" in math, and a "C" in economics. At that point, I didn't care as long as I passed. I really thought those classes were going to wipe me off the face of the planet.

In between the last two semesters before finishing up the bachelors degree, I had an appointment for my annual physical. I had lost 20 lbs which for my height and build was not a good thing. My blood pressure was that of a 12-year-old and my doctor could not understand how I was even walking, let alone, keeping on top of my insane responsibilities at work and home. Dr. Wilson said in his calm voice, "I think you may want to consider taking a break after this semester. This unhealthy schedule of a few hours of sleep and not enough to eat won't last very long." He went on to remind me that if we don't take care of our natural bodies with adequate sleep, a healthy diet and exercise, that the body will break down on us. Oh, by the way, I was still volunteering in the community because I had way too much pride and not enough wisdom to take a brief leave of absence. Although, I comprehended exactly what Dr. Wilson was saying, I was in such a trance and on auto pilot that, I dismissed his wise counsel and repeated the same dumb behaviors the next semester which fortunately, was the final semester. I just wanted to finish and be done with school for the moment.

Now that I look back, it wasn't such a great idea to take four classes during those last two semesters. But I was determined to get my bachelors by the end of my daughter's junior year in high school to ensure that she had the best senior year ever. I took her senior year off and enrolled in the MBA program the following year when she was a freshman in college. I figured by then, we would both benefit from us being in college at the same time. Some 18 months later, I finished the two-year MBA program. Upon completing my bachelor's and master's degrees, I reluctantly participated in the graduation ceremony. I just wanted my papers and had no desire to walk across the stage. Of course, my father would have something to say about this. He brought up the fact that Troy and I ran off to the justice of the peace to get married and robbed him of the opportunity to walk me down the aisle. Wow, Dad, lay on the guilt! Next, he reminded me that there were so many family members and friends who supported me on this journey, and he asked that I not rob them of the opportunity to see me walk across the stage. Who could argue with that?

Touchdown!

Not only did I walk both times, but I walked with honors and thankfully, my mom was alive to see it all. She got to see her constant words to me fulfilled: be a lifelong learner. No sooner than I graduated with honors from the MBA program, the school counselor called to advise me that I was four classes away from earning an executive graduate degree in Human Resources. I just couldn't get enough, so I signed up and took two classes over two semesters and walked away with those papers as well! On a side note, Troy and I renewed our wedding vows when we celebrated 20 years of marriage and had a full ceremony where my mom was present and my dad proudly walked me down the aisle!

As I reflect back on the days that I wanted to quit, not only did the poem about excuses keep flooding my mind but also the fact that this phase of life was only for a season. In my mind, how could I encourage my daughter to go to college and finish if I hadn't led by example? All I can say is that I am eternally grateful and thankful that I didn't quit, that I had folks all around me who kept me straight, and that God gave me the strength to finish and finish strong.

I think during this chapter of my life, I realized that sleep was overrated or at least that's what I told myself. At best, I would get 4-5 hours on any given night. To me, the sacrifice was worth the reward. You've heard it said that anything worth having is worth fighting for, and I've found that to be true. The biggest lesson and achievement for me during that time, in addition to the degrees, was finding the peace that came with my own version of "balance".

"Happiness cannot be far behind a grateful heart and a peaceful mind."

– Unknown

Essentially, each of us must come to terms with our own balance, be grateful for those in our lives that support us, live life with no regrets, and be at peace with the outcome.

How will you find and define your balance today?

....

....

....

....

....

....

Surround yourself with those on the same mission as you.

Sleep is Overrated

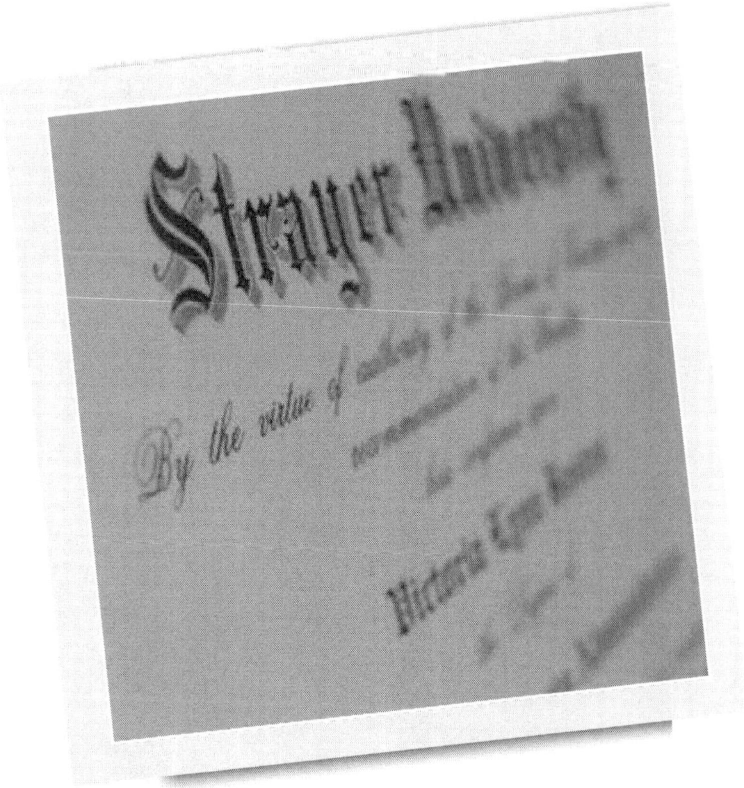

Actor, Will Smith with an estimated net worth of more than $250 million said that he excels in having a ridiculous, sickening, work ethic. When others are sleeping and eating, and a few are out partying, he can be found working.

I've come to realize that we make time for whatever is important to us. Simply put, whatever is worth having, we have to work and sacrifice for it. When I started my career more than 28 years ago, I knew from watching my mom and dad's insane work ethic that I, too, had to put the work in. I never saw mom or dad napping, goofing off, or wasting one second on anything that didn't benefit their family. While they were not wealthy by today's standard or stacked with material things, the unconditional love provided daily and wisdom imparted to me was and is priceless. I never saw any unproductive time and most impressively, they taught me how to make the time good and to make every second count. I'm sure they goofed off and had fun and I'm sure they didn't always make every second count. However, my overall recollection of my childhood home was one of productivity.

As the youngest of seven children, I was taught at a very young age that responsibility, accountability, and work were not bad words. In fact, they were indeed, words to live by. I think I may have actually taken the word "work" a little bit too literal upon high school graduation as I had no desire at the time to go off to college even though that was the expectation in my home.

You see, I had been working every summer since reaching the legal working age of 14, in a coveted summer job with the DC government. I continued to work every day after school throughout high school. Even though I knew my parents were a little disappointed in my decision to continue working full-time post-high school rather than going directly to college like most of my friends and older siblings, they supported me every step of the way. A big part of this decision to work right out of high school was also driven by the fact that, not long after graduation, I learned that I was pregnant with Danielle. It would have been a huge challenge to attend college full-time, work full-time, and raise a newborn simultaneously. Even though I didn't take the traditional path like my parents had hoped, they reminded me daily, that I could achieve anything that I put my mind to and was willing to work for. I can recall my dad sharing his hopes of me attending Hampton University and if not college, joining the Air Force since I often joked about joining the military. My mom rarely sugar-coated anything and simply told me that this road would be tough. But after all, I was built for tough times, she said. The coaching they gave me was straightforward: get a plan, work the plan and realize that I was now a parent and every decision from that day forward needed to have my child and her wellbeing in mind. They always kept in front of me that sacrifice was a requirement and prerequisite to success.

It was in my early days that I realized that sleep was in fact overrated. I found myself much like Will Smith in that while my high school peers were napping after school, I was working. When they slept in on Saturday mornings, I was off to work! When they were hopping from house party to house party on a Friday night, I was studying. Failing wasn't an option and to be able to attend high school and work full-time, I had to sacrifice something. Every so often I found time to go to a movie or attend the school dance, but the priority was to graduate with honors while working full-time, period. By having that Will Smith "sickening" work ethic in front of me all the days of my life by way of my parents, I was without excuse. As I continued to work full-time post high school, I realized that I had developed that sickening work ethic and made no apologies for it. I saw right off the break the incredible benefit and fruit it bore!

During my senior year in high school, I only needed two credits to graduate which afforded me a half-day schedule. I attended class in the morning and worked at the Department of Defense in the afternoons as part of the Washington, D.C., high school work program. Right after graduation, and even before I became pregnant, I was offered full-time employment with a step increase and promotion from a GS-2 to a GS-3. I thought I was big stuff and had convinced myself that I didn't need to worry about college. Not too long after accepting the Defense Department job, I learned that I was pregnant. So having the full-time job was perfect for us financially, in my mind. I think looking back, I allowed the pregnancy to convince me that I couldn't do both work and attend school with a new baby. In addition, my boyfriend (now husband) wasn't thrilled about raising a family in one of our parent's homes. Having a full-time job became my priority.

After Troy got over the initial shock that he was going to be a dad at the age of 23 and that he now would be responsible for just more than himself, our conversations began to shift and focus on the three of us. I was very torn about the idea of moving. When Danielle was born, we were both still living in our respective parent's homes. My mom and dad were very helpful at night, especially since I had to get up early in the morning for work. We had created a nursery for my daughter in my parent's home and they had become very attached. Any time they heard us discussing moving out, tension would rise and sparks would fly. Troy and my dad had a great relationship; however, the relationship between Troy and my mom at that time was another story.

She wasn't too happy with the thought of us moving out to where she considered "so far away." The apartment we were considering was less than 30 minutes away. Troy was determined to find us our own place and be the man that he was created to be. He assured me that we would be okay in the process. We were both willing to make the sacrifices necessary, including missing a few hours of sleep, to make it work. Day care was at Troy's grandmother's house in DC, which meant I would be driving in rush-hour traffic to drop Danielle off, dash to work and frequently travel in peak traffic in the evenings to pick her up on days when Troy worked late. I will admit that, although it was very scary in the beginning, Troy was true to his word then and has been every day since.

Making sacrifices

Whether it's work, your family, or anything else deemed important to you, I would admonish you to give and deliver your very best self. Sacrifices will need to be made, there is no side stepping.

I was raised to give my best and expected to be the best in everything I did, although that wasn't always the case. I was reminded from my parents, husband and even our pastor that I had purpose and others deserved my best self; it was just that simple. In order to walk in this, I had to make good choices.

Once again, I needed to make time for what was important. Having a demanding full-time job, being a wife and mom and at times, enrolled in school full-time, required incredible discipline and sacrifice. I quickly realized that sleep would be limited, but only for a season. Whenever I started a new job, took on a big project or needed to devote additional time to any area of my life, I found myself reminding my extended family and friends that during that particular season, I would have limited availability for things that didn't add true value to the cause, whatever the cause was at the moment. Essentially, the conversation would go something like this... "Hey guys, I've got papers to write and studying on tap, so please don't bother inviting me to the movies, parties, dinners, weddings or funerals for the next 18 months!" Of course, they knew I was sort of joking about the funeral comment, but I got the point across. I didn't have any discretionary time nor any energy to waste. I was about the business of producing best-in-class results at work, being there for my husband and daughter, doubling down to finish that degree, volunteering in the community or anything else that was important to me.

When I look back on the time that I accepted the challenge

from Kathy, the church choir director, to go back to school and to eliminate the excuses, I realize that I was building muscle memory needed to face subsequent challenges in my life. After accomplishing something that seemed a little out of reach, given all the balls I was juggling, the sacrifices made and sleep lost were certainly worth it!

What sacrifices are you willing to make today to achieve your goals?

"No alarm clock needed, my passion wakes me."

– Eric Thomas

3 Slow Nickels

The last time I checked, three slow nickels exceeded one quick dime any day of the week. Often times, I found myself going after the quick dime that wasn't sustainable nor fulfilling. As you see others around you getting new jobs, promotions or what seems to be exciting opportunities while your journey seemingly is taking a different and slower pace, it's hard to remember that three slow nickels always outpace one quick dime. The key to enjoying the journey is having patience and appreciation for every stage, every step, every turn, every detour, every setback, every comeback, every adversity, and every success experienced along the way.

The Chinese proverb, "Be not afraid of growing slowly, be afraid only of standing still" reminds me that all progress should be celebrated and that standing still is never an option. During my journey climbing the corporate ladder, I was frequently reminded by my mom, that my route may not be closely patterned after others and it's okay to make my own way. As a young, ambitious, passionate, energetic overachiever with the sincere desire to win and help others around me win, the quick dime always sounded good and the three slow nickels never made sense. Early in my career when I worked for the Department of Defense for three years, I was getting promoted every six months, which certainly built confidence. However, because of the quick moves, I wasn't able to learn from mistakes. By the time I realized my mistakes because I was already off to the next thing. When I moved on from the government to the private sector in the summer of 1990, I was thrilled about the $10,000 jump in pay but the promotions weren't as fast as in the government. Still, I received several promotions in my new job and was leading employees twice as old as I was before the age of 25. What I didn't realize then but know now is that by moving around fast (hence the quick dime), I wasn't paying attention to mistakes, learning from them and making necessary adjustments along the way. It caught up with me later when I was leading larger, more complex teams.

During one of my quick-dime moves, I had the pleasure of working for one of the smartest men in the industry, the late Daniel Felder. He would call me into his office, and although I was his top sales account manager, he saw the gaps in my professional growth and maturity. Even though he saw that I was exceeding my goals and proud of my #1 status, he also saw, was that I wasn't spending enough time learning the financial aspects of the deals and developing overall business acumen. When he took the time to enlighten me, my career movement slowed some but I found that I was more effective. He taught me different approaches to inspire my team and peers to deliver results without leading by fear and intimidation. I was so busy focused on the next gig and motivated to nail the current job, I didn't realize that I came across as a bulldog. Thankfully, many of my colleagues knew my intentions but I can only imagine those who didn't really know me must have thought I was one crazy woman on a mission.

It wasn't until others who had traveled before me, achieved what I desired and filled with wisdom began to pour into my life professionally and personally, that I realized the reward always accompanied the three slow nickels. Having the patience and perseverance to put the work in day in and day out when many around me did just enough to get by, started to pay off. I was able to focus on delivering best-in-class results with the ability to lap those results year after year versus chasing the next opportunity. Far too often, we can miss the incredible opportunities to learn, grow, develop, and stretch ourselves in the current position as a result of spending an inordinate amount of time running after the next big thing.

Take time to grow

I am a huge supporter of owning your own career, planning for it, charting the way, making the necessary connections and letting key stakeholders know what you want. But I am not a supporter of charting a career course that is paced so fast that you neglect your assignment or leave a trail of blood or cartilage behind. One wise person, my former director and now dear friend, Brenda Finch, once told me that it's mission critical to bloom where you're planted. In other words, do a great job in your current role, plan for the next move but do it in such a manner that it doesn't become a distraction or have a negative impact.

How are you currently blooming where you're planted?

....

....

....

What position do you currently have?

What position do you want?

What steps are you taking right now to make it a reality?

In what ways have you found yourself chasing the next big thing and putting yourself at risk for a quick dime that isn't sustainable versus securing three slow nickels?

James A. Garfield put it this way: "Be fit for more than the thing you are now doing. Let everyone know that you have a reserve in yourself; that you have more power than you are now using. If you are not too large for the place you occupy, you are too small for it."

"I've missed more than 9000 shots in my career. I've lost almost 300 games, 26 times I've been trusted to take the game winning shot and missed. I've failed over and over and over again in my life and that is why I succeed."

– Michael Jordan

Finish Strong

Photo: My parents in 2014, after 64 years of marriage. This is what commitment looks like.

Zig Ziglar reminds us, "Where you start is not as important as where you finish." You see, I used to be very insecure based on my starting point in my adult life. After all, I did not go off to college post-high school like most of my friends and siblings. In addition, my precious daughter was birthed out of wedlock. Certainly, my non-traditional start did not set me up for long-term success based on society's standards. Troy was 23 years old and I was 19. We experienced first hand the challenges of raising a child at such a young age, including enduring the naysayers. There were many out there who had already written us off and told us that we wouldn't make it. I can remember primarily older co-workers who seemed to prejudge whether we could be successful as a family and essentially said, "This will never work."

The assumption was that Troy wouldn't step up to the plate, and we would become another statistic of a single mom and deadbeat dad with baby-mama drama. We were determined for that NOT to be our story. Funny enough, those who never believed in us are nowhere to be found and those family and close friends who cheered us on, coached us, prayed for us, and encouraged us every step of the way, remain in our lives today. You see, Troy worked full-time during the day and attended college classes in the evening. I figured I would just work full-time and not even try to attend school with everything that I was facing at the time.

My start wasn't so ideal and I had plenty of older adults frequently reminding me that to be successful in life, I should have attended college after high school, and should have waited until I was in my late twenties or thirties to get married and start a family. The way I saw it, I had two choices in front of me: I could either believe success wasn't an option based on my seemingly rocky start or believe that I could redirect my focus and energy and change the trajectory for my life.

Interestingly enough, there were always great examples in front of me and around me to show me what was possible, if only I was willing to change my perspective and see through different lenses.

My most favorite part of the working world was and still is, leading and inspiring others to achieve the impossible. Seeing the light bulbs go off in others is most energizing and rewarding. My own insecurities and self-doubt early in my career stemmed from the fact that most of my peers and leaders had college degrees and I didn't. Now I know first-hand the feeling when you achieve a goal you never thought possible. Deep down inside, I knew that I came from a family of champions and winners, but the negative thoughts that I allowed to roam free in my mind seemed to slow me down and sometimes had me off course. It wasn't until others around me, who saw something in me that I didn't see in myself, challenged me to walk in purpose and embrace my potential that my career took off. Even after several promotions, I made rookie mistakes like not being sensitive to the needs of my team and putting work and results first above everything else. Thankfully, by then, I was very open to feedback and had a sincere desire to be better every day than the day before.

In order to finish something, you have to resolve in your mind and in your heart that it's worth the fight. Anything worth having is worth fighting for. For me, finishing is a mindset, it's a state of being. Mahatma Gandhi summed it up this way:

"Your beliefs become your thoughts,
Your thoughts become your words,
Your words become your actions,
Your actions become your habits,
Your habits become your values,
Your values become your destiny."

We all know that it's much easier to quit, but the nice thing is that when you get in the habit of finishing everything you start, no matter how big or small, you become a finisher in every aspect of your life.

I will tell you what I would frequently tell the new hires:

There will be some days that will be more challenging than others. There will be some customers that seem impossible to service. There will be co-workers that you honestly believe were sent on earth to make your day a living hell. There will be bosses that you will wonder, *how in the world did they ever make it into leadership?* I'm sure you can think of few to add to the list as well.

Find that person, place, or thing that drives you. Put a picture of this person, place or thing on the back side of your badge which you're likely to always have on in the office. Let this be a constant reminder of why you must finish. Let it remind you why it's imperative to finish and why quitting can never be an option. Let it remind you why you get out of bed day in and day out.

I always had a picture of my daughter on the back of my badge. It was the one thing that reminded me that no matter how tough things got or how hot the fire became, I had to finish so that she would have a chance at a better life. She never knew that her picture was on the back of my badge. I'm sure had she known it, she may have been mortified to know that her mommy carried a picture of her from age 1 until age 26. It was my constant reminder that I had to finish and finish strong.

Stay for the long-haul

I can honestly say that I didn't have to look very far for great examples of finishers. My husband's grandparents' 73-year marriage, finished strong. My mother- and father-in-law were married for 45 years before she passed. They finished strong. I realized that they were teaching everyone fortunate enough to be in their great company how important it is to finish and finish strong.

My parents were married 64 years before my mom passed Oct. 12, 2014, due to complications with dementia. Although her memory was still pretty sharp in the year leading up to her passing, she was unable to really care for herself. I watched my dad, who has a bad back, lift my mom every morning and night as he bathed her, fed her, and got her out of bed and into her reclining chair. He never once complained. In fact, he looked forward to caring for her in such a meticulous way. We often reminded him that the nurse really did know what she was doing; it became our inside joke and the incredible nursing staff went along for the ride! He refused to leave her side and I am grateful that he was right there when she took her last breath. If up to that point I hadn't picked up on how to have a lasting relationship, watching my parents live out their vows – 'til death do us part — taught me more than I could ever learn about what commitment was really all about. I got a first-hand lesson on what it means to finish strong in marriage.

The key to all of their successful marriages was never quitting. Finish what you start!

Though I had great examples around me, I also didn't have to look very far for quitters and haters either. They absolutely made their presence known all day, every day. There will always be competing voices. The critical question is, which voice will you listen to? Which example will you follow? Will you be willing to put the work in to finish and finish strong?

When I announced my retirement after 25 years, I made sure that as I exited stage left, that I hung up my jersey as the #1 Area Vice President of Customer Service in the nation. In fact, I was the first African-American to ever serve in that position. It was a strong finish!

You see, I never thought any of this was possible based on my humble beginnings. As I celebrate 25 years of marriage and an incredible 25 year career, I look back with pride on achievements in my personal and professional life. I am especially proud of my daughter who finished college in three years and is now married and leading a non-profit organization with her husband, serving the youth of Compton (www.discoverYOUcompton.org). I can truly say, finishing strong pays big dividends!

At the beginning of this chapter, I quoted Zig Ziglar's reminder that where you start is not as important as where you finish. He also has pointed out, "Outstanding people have one thing in common: an absolute sense of mission."

How can you get laser-focused on your mission and busy finishing what you started today?

....

....

....

....

....

....

....

....

"It's kind of fun to do the impossible."

—Walt Disney

The Best is Yet to Come

Photo: Danielle and Dion Watson, expecting Baby Watson in june 2016.

As is customary with any team that I have had the privilege of serving, I make a commitment to invest in their leadership and professional development. In my last assignment before retiring, I was fortunate enough to have responsibility for more than 5,000 employees which included hundreds of supervisors and associate directors in addition to my direct reports which also consisted of 11 directors and an executive assistant.

Each year I, along with a few of my support staff, would review my vision for the annual leadership summit and all the associated moving parts. It was a huge undertaking as my team was spread out from Maine to Alabama. It wasn't always easy to bring the leaders to a central location for a few days of development and in some cases we did just that and in other times, we suitcased the summit and took it on the road to each of the locations.

For the Spring 2015 leadership summits, we packaged a robust agenda with incredibly talented, experienced and brilliant speakers who were all members of my leadership team and hit the road! It was two full weeks of back-to-back travel up and down the east coast with the team; I enjoyed every minute. We spent several hours in the car driving from one location to the next and we learned a great deal from one another. This was one of my most favorite times of the year. This time, I asked one of my managers to present on a topic, and while she was delighted for the opportunity, the timing wasn't the best as she was caring for a sick parent at the time. However, as any responsible leader would do, she didn't leave me hanging. In fact, she recommended one of her peers to present on a very hot topic: employee engagement. This was perfect on so many fronts. For starters, her peer was a newer manager within the organization and had a very critical role. She was responsible for ensuring my organization's attendance was best-in-class, that employee attrition lowered and overall employee satisfaction improved as well as helping drive meaningful employee engagement in general.

I think anyone would agree that her role was essential to our team's success. It was a no-brainer to have this new manager hit the road with us and become one of the leadership summit presenters. While her presentation and call to action regarding employee engagement was a big hit, and the managers in attendance at the summits took away actionable best practices that they could immediately implement to improve results, she was also a hit during the leadership panel discussion that I had the pleasure of moderating.

The topic of making gutsy moves in our careers came up in every one of our leadership panel discussions. I moderated the panel and along with the attendees was super-charged by each of the leadership discussions. There was one question the new manager posed to the audience at every summit: What would you do if you were not afraid? Every time that question was raised, I thought to myself, *Wow, that's a great question for the audience!* I got super excited each time and couldn't wait to hear the responses from the audience. A few leaders said they would take on different jobs that required them to relocate their families if they were not afraid. Others said they would go back to school and complete their degrees, start their own business, etc. Although I was fascinated by the question and responses, I never entertained the question for myself.

What if I wasn't afraid?

Months later, I watched my daughter and son-in-law pour their heart and soul into their non-profit — Discover YOU Compton, Inc. They have paused very successful professional dancing and acting careers to launch their social justice, arts and education non-profit. And that's when I realized, working on behalf of our youth is something I would do if I were not afraid to leave my comfortable, familiar, seemingly secure, and overall successful 25-year career at Verizon.

And so it came to be that in July 2015, an opportunity presented itself where I could, in fact, retire after 25 amazing years at what I believed was the best company in the entire world. After all, this career afforded me so many opportunities to care for my immediate and extended family in ways I never thought possible. Why in the world would I ever consider another option?

So here I am, doing exactly the things that I was afraid to do: writing my first book, supporting my daughter's non-profit full time, continuing to serve on the National Network to End Domestic Violence board, volunteering in the community, helping young leaders get established and spending precious time with my family.

Whatever stage of life you are in, wherever you are in your professional career, understand that the best is always to come. Appreciate where you are now, but know that it's a journey. While the phases of my life that I shared throughout this book are mostly behind me, there's still more life ahead of me. I encourage you to embrace your future just as I'm doing. You may reach a point or have already reached a point where you need to answer the same question that I found myself answering not too long ago: *What would I do if I were not afraid?* If you're like me, analytical and detailed oriented, you may want all the details laid out as the unknown can be frightening. Now that I'm actively in what I would describe as Act II of my life, the unknown is still somewhat scary but the hope that I have reminds me, "It's all good." You, too, may be at a crossroads in your life. Well, stop stressing and enjoy the journey! The Second Act may be your best one yet.

I will admit that I am not exactly sure of how my Second Act will develop, or the array of professional opportunities that will arise. However, what I am well assured of is the very fact that the best is yet to come for me and you!

What would you do if you weren't afraid? What's holding you back? It's time to journal and face your fears head-on so that you too will overcome them.

....

....

"You can't start the next chapter of your life if you keep re-reading the last one."

Photo: My dad and I. #ageisjustanumber

Acknowledgments

My dad, Ellsworth Hutchinson, Jr. — you knew all along that I had a book on the inside of me and you are the one who inspired me to pause and share my story so that I may inspire others! Thank YOU!

My sisters, Donna Marshall and Dana Hutchinson — you pushed me, encouraged me and cheered me on along the way. Nothing like sisters!

My nephew and niece, Ryan and Sara Hutchinson — you stayed up with me for two nights in a row brainstorming the title! I sure do appreciate you guys!

My middle brother, David Hutchinson, the private investigator — you kept me on track by calling periodically to interrogate me. Love you lots!

My oldest brother, Ronald Hutchinson — surprise! I kept this a secret from you! Sorry!

My amazing in-laws and other nephews and nieces, Lisa Hutchinson, Shellye Hutchinson, Lawrence Marshall, Robert Murray III, Lauren Coyle, Josh Coyle, Jasmine Ray, and Brittany Hutchinson — you continue to be my raving fans. Love you to the moon and back!

Mark & Bea Dabney and Clint & Yodi Crouch – the best cousins and friends $$$$ could buy!

My incredible daughter, Danielle Jai (Boston) Watson and selfless son-in-law, Dion Watson — you call me your hero, but you haven't quite realized yet, that you are in fact my heroes! Unlimited hugs & kisses!

My best friend, lover, confidant, life partner, father of my amazing daughter, my personal comedian and husband of 25 incredible years, Troy Pernell Boston — you are the reason I wake up every day and give my very best self to the world in which we live. Endless love – xoxoxoxoxo!

Special thanks to all who have poured into my life both professionally and personally. I had three extra special bosses who were divinely placed in my life at various stages — almost strategically:

Brenda Finch, my first customer service and sales director back in the 90s. You didn't pull any punches. I am so grateful that you and I remain close and often laugh about the time that you said to me, after I repeatedly brought problems about the work environment to your attention… "Vicky, since you have so much mouth, so much to say and can point out all the problems, how about you get into a leadership position and help affect change." In less than six months, I was promoted into management.

Eric Cevis, you were vice president of large business internet sales at the time that I convinced myself that I wasn't cut out for the corporate account executive sales position in your organization. I let you know, 30 days after accepting the promotion, I was going to retreat back to my previous position where I was very comfortable. You came from behind your desk, sat right next to me at the round table in his office and said… "No Vicky, you are not going to go back to your old position. That would mean that you are quitting and winners don't quit." I thanked you for your time, returned to my office, got out of my feelings, asked my peers for help and finished that year #1 in the nation as the 1st African-American female internet sales account manager. Thank you for believing in me.

Andrea Custis, my Vice President before retiring in 2011 — you had a real appreciation for my talent, tenacity, natural ability to lead and inspire. Your real desire to get the best out of others, pushed me far beyond what I ever thought possible. You constantly reminded me that… "Vicky, you were built for this, there's no one better" and you inspired me to go hard every day and most importantly, to finish strong.

Matt Patterson — for sharing your incredibly inspiring story, *My Emily,* with me that put me in high gear.

My coach, Jonathan Sprinkles — for reminding me that "It CAN Be Done."

Delina Pryce McPhaull — for keeping me on my toes throughout the entire publishing process. Amazing!

Gratitude changes everything. I am forever grateful.

About the Author

Victoria L. Boston currently serves as the Director of Community Relations for Discover.YOU Compton Inc., a social justice non-profit organization bringing arts and education to underserved youth in Compton, CA.

Boston has 35+ years of corporate and community leadership experience with proven success at every stage of the game. Her energy and passion to connect others to what's possible is unmatched. She holds an MBA in Marketing, Bachelors in Business, Executive Graduate degree in Human Resources, Project Management Certificate; has countless hours of executive leadership development from Columbia University Graduate School of Business and is a graduate of the Master Series for Distinguished Leaders in Washington, D.C. Coupled with firsthand experience, she delights to share her keys to success with others. The road Boston has traveled is full of lessons learned from mistakes made, setbacks and comebacks, and is loaded with priceless, yet timeless nuggets to help others reach their potential as they travel on their own journey.

An inspirational leader, author, speaker, coach, and community volunteer, she has the natural ability to influence and inspire greatness in those she encounters. Boston has the unique gift of connecting with diverse audiences, displaying total transparency while remaining authentic. She has electrified so many across the country ranging from elementary school students, colleges, churches, nonprofit organizations and in corporate settings for intimate groups with as few as 10 and as large as 20,000 attendees of all ages at the Mercedes Benz Superdome in New Orleans, LA.

A humble recipient of many honors, she has been awarded the prestigious Verizon CEO Leadership Excellence Award for exceptional results, the National Diversity Award, and the Dr. Martin Luther King, Jr. Leadership Award for her commitment to the professional development of others. In addition, she received a Certificate of Appreciation from the United States Department of Agriculture for her significant contributions to their EEOAC Women's History Month celebration, was the keynote speaker at the University of North Carolina Wilmington College, Office of Institutional Diversity and Inclusion annual conference. She has been a three-time guest speaker at Strayer University for the school of business as well as a keynote speaker at a Strayer commencement ceremony. Recognized for her outstanding support of the Maryland Business Roundtable for Education Achievement Counts Program, Boston has been a guest speaker on multiple occasions at the Francis Scott Key Middle School's Career Day, and twice acknowledged for her leadership from Michelle Ebanks, President of Essence Communications. Celebrated as Verizon's Women "Making History Now" campaign and "Don't Just Celebrate History, Create It" Black History Month honoree, she has also been featured twice for her contributions in the local community in the Baltimore Afro American newspaper in which her late maternal grandmother, Constance Eleanor Daniel was one of the first African-American female journalists.

Boston is an active member at her local church, From the Heart Church Ministries in Suitland, MD, and serves on the Board of Directors for Discover YOU Compton Inc. in Compton, CA, the National Network to End Domestic Violence (NNEDV) and The Skills Society Foundation in Washington, D.C.

Keep in Touch!

I would love to hear from you.

Victoria

www.VictoriaBoston.com

bostonvictoria

Made in the USA
Middletown, DE
27 July 2025

10609985R00073